Workbook

For

Fight Right

How Successful Couples Turn Conflict into Connection

(An Implementation Guide To Julie Schwartz Gottman Phd, John Gottman Phd's Book With Over 70 Practical And Reflective Questions)

By

Wing Prints

INTRODUCTION

This workbook doesn't just teach us how to fight right but also teaches us how to successfully turn our conflicts into connections in relationships, and how to find immediate relief in relationships.

It also highlights the reason why couples fight, why couples fight the way they do, and what they fight about in the first part of the book. The second part of the book discusses the anatomy of a fight from beginning to end, the common mistakes we make as couples, and how to prevent a regrettable incident from becoming another regrettable incident.

Use the practical and reflective questions as an implementation guide or journal to understand the conflicts in your relationships and turn them into connections.

PART I

CONFLICT 101

Why We Fight

Objectives

1. To understand the reason why we fight.

2. To highlight ways for couples who are struggling to get immediate relief.

3. To understand the benefits of conflict.

Summary

The chapter discusses ways we can use to get immediate relief if we are struggling in a relationship, how AI can be used for coding conflict, and how to code our emotions during a fight. It also talks about how personality differences, major life changes, and life stress can make couples fight, and how negative emotions can escalate conflict no matter the reason for it. It further highlights that conflict is part of life emphasizing that early conflict in relationships doesn't mean the relationship will have a bad outcome and low-conflict relationships are more fragile. It concludes by highlighting the reason why we fight, how to address conflict, and the benefits of conflict emphasizing that the goal of conflict is mutual understanding so we should approach our partner with curiosity and not anger.

Lessons

1. Therapists are trained to look for subtle cues in body language and physiology, vocal tone, language choices, etc.

2. Computer (AI) can be programmed to code conflict.

3. How couples behave in conflict can affect their relationship in the future.

4. Perpetual problems between partners typically stem from differences in personality and lifestyle preferences.

5. Major life changes like becoming parents and life stress are some of the reasons why we fight.

6. Anger is an approach emotion, the more terrified we are of anger, the more polarized we become.

7. Early conflict in a relationship doesn't necessarily mean the relationship will not last long.

8. When conflict was driven by the female partner bringing up issues, the relationship turned out to be a stronger and more successful one.

Questions

1. What made the researchers to develop a new platform for couples struggling in their relationships?

_____

_____

_____

_____

_____

_____

_____

2. Is it possible for AI to mimic the role of a skilled therapist during conflict resolution, if yes, how?

_____

_____

_____

_____

_____

_____

_____

3. According to the authors, what specific coding system was used by John Gottman and his team to analyze couples' interactions?

_____

_____

_____

_____

_____

_____

_____

4. Based on this chapter, what are the key elements of conflict identified in the textbook fight?

_____

_____

_____

_____

_____

_____

_____

5. How do biological factors contribute to conflicts in relationships according to the study on sense of smell and attraction?

_____

_____

_____

_____

_____

_____

_____

6. What effect does stress from external factors like work spill over into marital interactions?

_____

_____

_____

_____

_____

_____

_____

7. Why can it be said that early conflict in relationships correlates with long-term relationship satisfaction?

_____

_____

_____

_____

_____

_____

_____

8. From your point of view, how can you explain the concept of the "wife negative effect"?

_____

_____

_____

_____

_____

_____

_____

9. How is it beneficial to approach conflict with curiosity rather than contempt or criticism?

_____

_____

_____

_____

_____

_____

_____

10. Explain the term "conflict culture" as described in the chapter and what significance is it in relationships.

_____

_____

_____

_____

_____

_____

Why We Fight the Way We Fight

Objectives

1. To understand why we fight the way we do.

2. To understand how our beliefs can start or stop the conflict.

3. To build awareness of the critical factors that shape how we fight.

Summary

This chapter discusses the reason why we fight the way we do, the different types of fighting styles within a healthy partnership which are conflict-avoidant couples (avoiders shy away from active conflict), validating couples (they do disagree, and they aren't afraid to get into it), and volatile couple (their fights immediately move into a heated debate, with high emotion and raised voices, but often with a lot of humor and positivity as well), the need for ratio in conflict style, and the required ratio for each conflict style emphasizing that any of the three main conflict styles can be happy and successful, providing they keep that math equation healthy. It further talks about what meta-emotion is and the disadvantages of meta-emotion mismatch, the stages of a fight (build an agenda, persuasion, and compromise), and how we can change our conflict style.

Lessons

1. Conflict-avoidant couples tend not to have conflictual discussions at all, preferring to "agree to disagree" and keep the peace rather than get mired in a potentially upsetting conversation.

2. Validators fight, but they fight politely, discussing issues collaboratively, and are interested in finding a compromise.

3. Volatile couples erupt into conflict more frequently, burn hotter, and are generally more intense and dramatic.

4. The secret to almost at-conflict style is the magic ratio.

5. Conflict has a purpose and can lead to great things, but it's not going to be all rainbows and roses while you're getting there.

6. Any of the three main conflict styles can be happy and successful, providing they keep that math equation healthy.

7. Meta-emotion is how we feel about feelings.

8. Understanding your style and your partner's style builds empathy and compassion, which means that even a fight can become a safe enough space for you to explore your issues together and do something crucial.

Questions

1. How does our conflict style affect how we typically approach disagreements?

_____

_____

_____

_____

_____

_____

_____

2. How does the way validating couples approach conflict resolution differ from avoidant couples?

_____

_____

_____

_____

_____

_____

_____

3. According to the chapter, what is the "magic ratio" in conflict resolution and how can it affect the way we react in conflict?

_____

_____

_____

_____

_____

_____

4. Based on the chapter, how can couples improve their conflict resolution skills, regardless of their conflict style?

_____

_____

_____

_____

_____

_____

5. What are the characteristics of the people with volatile conflict styles according to the chapter?

_____

_____

_____

_____

_____

_____

6. From your understanding of the chapter, explain the concept of "meta-emotion mismatch" and how can meta-emotion mismatches affect the communication between partners during conflicts.

_____

_____

_____

_____

_____

_____

7. Explain the communication patterns of a validator-volatile couple as described in this text.

_____

_____

_____

_____

_____

_____

8. What is the correlation between intent and impact during conflict conversations?

_____

_____

_____

_____

_____

_____

_____

9. How do conflict styles differ in their approach to persuasion?

_____

_____

_____

_____

_____

_____

10. If conflict styles can be changed, what strategies do you suggest for couples who are looking to modify their approach to conflict?

_____

_____

_____

_____

_____

_____

What We Fight About

Objectives

1. To know what couples fight about.

2. To correct some misconceptions about conflict.

3. To educate readers on how to fight right.

Summary

This chapter discusses what couples fight about with the first one being nothing, how and why ecstasy can turn into eggshells. It also discusses what a bid for connection is, ways that partners tend to respond to each other's bids for connection, andthe two types of fights which are solvable (has a solution and can be resolved) and perpetual (cannot be resolved). It further talks about how negative emotions can escalate conflict, the meaning of gridlock, and how we can get out of it. It concludes by correcting some myths of conflict, highlighting some relationship deal breakers (abuse, refusing to seek help for addiction, and differences surrounding having children), and teaching us how to fight right.

Lessons

1. The number 1 thing couples fight about is nothing.

2. A big part of satisfying long-term love is developing the capacity to realize when what we're fighting about is not cold pizza but a longing for efforts to be appreciated; not a plant but the pressures of new commitment and not having the space to talk about it; not the price of a bottle of wine but a deep fear of parental rejection.

3. A bid for connection is anything you do or your partner does to try to get the other person's attention and connection with them.

4. Solvable fights can feel pretty bad, especially when we're making some common conflict mistakes.

5. When negative emotions aren't listened to, they intensify, because we can't get our partner's attention.

6. Approach conflict differently, at a fundamental level, not how to solve one particular fight.

7. Conflict is unavoidable, even for the happiest of couples.

8. Never express anger by aiming contempt or criticism at your partner.

Questions

1. From your experience, what are the most common examples of conflicts that couples normally face?

_____

_____

_____

_____

_____

_____

_____

2. How do conflicts progress within a relationship?

_____

_____

_____

_____

_____

_____

_____

3. Explain the concept of "bids for connection" as mentioned in the chapter and how do partners respond to each other's bids for connection.

_____

_____

_____

_____

_____

_____

4. Based on the chapter, why do bids for connection matter in a relationship?

_____

_____

_____

_____

_____

_____

5. How do you suggest we address perpetual conflicts within a relationship?

_____

_____

_____

_____

_____

_____

6. What is gridlock, how does it manifest in a relationship, and how can couples to handle conflicts that become gridlocked?

_____

_____

_____

_____

_____

_____

7. How do you know that a couple might be experiencing gridlock in their relationship?

_____

_____

_____

_____

_____

_____

8. How can our deeper dreams and desires contribute to our conflict with our partner?

_____

_____

_____

_____

_____

_____

9. As described in the chapter, explain the concept of "dreams within conflict"?

_____

_____

_____

_____

_____

_____

10. From your point of view, what are the deal-breakers in relationships?

_____

_____

_____

_____

_____

_____

PART II

The Five Fights Everybody Has

FIGHT # 1: THE BOMB DROP

Mistake: Starting Off Wrong

Objectives

1. To highlight the mistakes we make in conflict.

2. To understand how we can get off on the right foot

3. To educate readers on how to make amends for past mistakes.

Summary

This chapter talks about a narrow and critical window of opportunity emphasizing that it takes 180 seconds to get off on the right or wrong foot, common mistakes like harsh start up that couples tend to make, the qualities of the mistakes, why harsh start-up is a common mistake, factors that fuels harsh start-up like stress, resentment, turning away, and we don't know any better, and the disadvantages of harsh start-up. It further highlights how we can get off on the right foot, the power of persuasion, the need for softened start-ups, and how we can makeharsh start-ups softer.

Lessons

1. It takes 180 seconds to get off on the right foot.

2. it's not about conflict style (volatility), it's about the ratio of positive to negative interactions.

3. There is no such thing as constructive criticism. Criticism is always destructive.

4. Don't store up complaints and resentments. Tackle them as they arise.

5. Couples who use softened start-ups have a much greater chance of success in their relationship.

6. A softened start-up is a powerful indicator that a couple is going to be successful in the long term.

7. A universal quality of masters of love: they start with kindness even when they're upset.

8. Success in this context is not just staying together but also experiencing high levels of happiness and satisfaction.

Questions

1. Why is the first three minutes in a conflict discussionsignificant, according to the chapter?

   _____

   _____

   _____

   _____

   _____

   _____

   _____

2. What are the key traits of a harsh start-up in a conflict?

   _____

   _____

   _____

   _____

   _____

   _____

   _____

3. What is the difference between criticism and productive complaint in conflict?

_____

_____

_____

_____

_____

_____

_____

_____

4. What is the effect of stress on harsh start-ups in relationships?

_____

_____

_____

_____

_____

_____

_____

_____

5. How can we improve a conflict discussion that had a harsh start-up?

_____

_____

_____

_____

_____

_____

_____

_____

6. How do successful couples handle conflict differently from others?

_____

_____

_____

_____

_____

_____

_____

_____

7. Why is it important to postpone persuasion in conflict resolution?

_____

_____

_____

_____

_____

_____

_____

8. How can softened start-ups improve communication during conflicts?

_____

_____

_____

_____

_____

_____

_____

9. According to the chapter, what are the three essential components of a successful softened start-up?

_____

_____

_____

_____

_____

_____

_____

10. In what way can conflict styles influence the expression of softened start-ups?

_____

_____

_____

_____

_____

_____

_____

FIGHT # 2: THE FLOOD

Mistake: Attacking, Defending, Withdrawing

Objectives

1. To create awareness of the concept of 'flood'.

2. To understand how to start on the right track.

3. To understand how we can solve the moment, identify and express our needs, and repair our relationship.

Summary

This chapter discusses flooding and its disadvantages emphasizing that it happens when we get overwhelmed in conflict, hijacked by our nervous system in response to negativity from our partners. It also talks about how we stay on the right track, how we can stop floods, how we can solve the moment, and the need for us to express our needs in a relationship. It talks about techniques (truth exercise) we can use to identify our needs, small repairs that can prevent major damage, and the need for repair.

Lessons

1. When you get flooded, you become incapable of fighting right.

2. There is no way to have a productive or positive conflict conversation once you're flooded.

3. Flooding shows up differently in all of us in terms of behavior, intensity, and timing.

4. During a fight, you don't have to solve the whole conflict. Just solve the moment.

5. Proprioception refers to your awareness of what's physically happening in your body.

6. A repair attempt in conflict is any comment or action that counteracts the negativity in a fight and prevents a conversation from escalating.

7. One of the saddest reasons why couples split is when they never quite manage to get aligned on repairs, when one person attempts, the other is closed off to it or misses it completely, and vice versa.

8. In conflict, your mission is to allow yourself to be vulnerable to turn attack and defend into self-disclosure and openness.

Questions

1. How do you know that you might be experiencing flooding during a conflict with your partner?

   _____

   _____

   _____

   _____

   _____

   _____

2. What role do physiological responses like increased heart rate and sweaty palms playin flooding during a heated conversation?

   _____

   _____

   _____

   _____

   _____

   _____

3. Has there ever been a scenario where flooding affected your ability to communicate effectively with your partner during a conflict?

_____

_____

_____

_____

_____

_____

4. What strategies can couples use to cope with flooding and prevent it from escalating a conflict further?

_____

_____

_____

_____

_____

_____

5. How can identifying the early signs of flooding help couples navigate difficult conversations?

_____

_____

_____

_____

_____

_____

6. How can the physiological effects of flooding impact a couple's ability to engage in rational communication during a conflict?

_____

_____

_____

_____

_____

_____

7. Why do we need to refrain from trying to get in the last word before taking a break during conflict?

_____

_____

_____

_____

_____

_____

8. According to the chapter, why is planning out arguments and rebuttals discouraged during conflicts?

_____

_____

_____

_____

_____

_____

9. What is the difference between volatile couples and validators in terms of experiencing flooding during conflicts?

_____

_____

_____

_____

_____

_____

_____

10. Based on the chapter, how does the quality of connection between partners influence the success of repair attempts during conflicts?

_____

_____

_____

_____

_____

_____

_____

FIGHT # 3: THE SHALLOWS

Mistake: Skimming the Surface

Objectives

1. To understand the need to dig deeper in conflict

2. To understand how to dream in conflict.

3. To educate readers on how conflict can lead to intimacy.

Summary

The chapter discusses common mistakes like skimming the surface that people make as a couple, how to know that you are making that mistake, signs that you need to dig deeper, how to dig deeper, and what happens when you dig deeper. It also talks about how conflict can lead to intimacy, how to practice dreams within conflict, the importance of practicing dreams within conflict, how to make space for your dream to surface, and how achieving your dream can help you in conflict.

Lessons

1. Dialogue calmly and constructively with one another when your differences come up.

2. You can't solve anything until you understand your partner's approach to this issue on a deeper level.

3. The worst conflict is the greatest opportunity for intimacy.

4. The more you and your partner talk about your respective goals, both big and small, and about your visions for the kind of life you want to have, the less you'll find yourselves in damaging conflicts fueled by unacknowledged or tamped-down dreams.

5. In relationship, understanding must precede resolution.

6. There's a wealth of knowledge we can come to understand about each other, which can truly be relationship-changing and life-changing.

7. Dreams in opposition can be a deal-breaker and vice versa.

8. You don't have to have the same "big life dream" to have a wonderful, fulfilling, and successful relationship.

Questions

1. How can our attempt to address our desires in a relationship cause conflict?

   _____

   _____

   _____

   _____

   _____

   _____

2. How do a couple's different conflict styles contribute to the gridlock in their relationship?

   _____

   _____

   _____

   _____

   _____

   _____

3. What are the signs that indicates that a couple needs to delve deeper into their conflict instead of skimming the surface?

_____

_____

_____

_____

_____

_____

_____

4. How can our dreams within conflict helpcouples understand each other's perspectives better? Give example.

_____

_____

_____

_____

_____

_____

_____

5. How can our experiences and upbringing influence or shape our views in relationships?

_____

_____

_____

_____

_____

_____

_____

6. According to the chapter, how did Shanae's upbringing influence her perception of love and the importance of receiving gifts?

_____

_____

_____

_____

_____

_____

7. In what ways does the contrasting childhood experiences between couple contribute to the conflicts in their relationship?

_____

_____

_____

_____

_____

_____

_____

8. Of what significance is our ability to trust and accept love from others to our relationship?

_____

_____

_____

_____

_____

_____

_____

9. In a relationship, what strategies can we implement to address our conflicting views and overcome the underlying emotional barriers to understanding each other's perspectives?

_____

_____

_____

_____

_____

_____

10. What impact did dreams within conflict have on the relationship dynamics?

_____

_____

_____

_____

_____

_____

FIGHT # 4: THE STANDOFF

Mistake: Competing to Win

Objectives

1. To understand the disadvantages of competing to win in relationships.

2. To understand the concept of 'yielding to win' in relationships.

3. To educate readers on the importance of trust, commitment, and accepting influence in a relationship.

Summary

This chapter talks about another mistake we make as a couple: competing to win, the disadvantages of the win-lose dynamic, and how to arrive at a place of cooperative gain. It also talks about gender, sexuality, and accepting influence, the need to accept influence, the gain in true compromise, how to know when the fight means the end, how to move from a zero-sum dynamic to Nash equilibrium, and the importance of trust and commitment in a relationship.

Lessons

1. If you want to "win" in a partner conflict, you need to yield some ground.

2. The more you allow yourself to be influenced by your partner, the more capacity you will have to influence them.

3. Accepting influence means being open to your partner's ideas and being willing to change your perspective as you learn more about how they feel and why.

4. When you can't be moved or influenced, you lose all power in the relationship.

5. The only way to become powerful in a relationship is to be capable of accepting influence. It's only when there's a true give-and-take that a person has real power.

6. In relationships, we are not opponents.

7. Our capacity to compromise successfully comes from trust and commitment.

8. Nobody is perfect, we all have flaws. You can work at rebuilding your trust and commitment in a relationship.

Questions

1. Based on the chapter, how does the concept of a "zero-sum outcome" apply to conflicts in intimate partner relationships?

_____

_____

_____

_____

_____

_____

_____

2. Why are some situations perceived as "zero-sum" even when they are not?

_____

_____

_____

_____

_____

_____

3. How do a couple's conflicting dreamsillustrate the challenges of compromise in relationships?

_____

_____

_____

_____

_____

_____

_____

4. What are the disadvantages of maintaining a zero-sum dynamic in a relationship over time?

_____

_____

_____

_____

_____

_____

_____

5. Explain the concept of "yielding to win" and how it applies to conflict resolution in a relationship?

_____

_____

_____

_____

_____

_____

_____

6. According to the author, how can the refusal to accept influenceimpact one's power in a relationship?

_____

_____

_____

_____

_____

_____

7. Why did the author emphasize the importance of accepting influence in a relationship?

_____

_____

_____

_____

_____

_____

8. Considering the chapter, how does the Bagel Method aim to facilitate compromise in conflicts between couples?

_____

_____

_____

_____

_____

_____

9. How can a couple reach a compromise that satisfies both partners?

_____

_____

_____

_____

_____

_____

_____

10. What is the significance of trust and commitment in resolving conflicts and reaching compromises in relationships?

_____

_____

_____

_____

_____

_____

FIGHT # 5: THE CHASM IN THE ROOM

Mistake: Stewing About the Fight

Objectives

1. To understand the need to process fights.

2. To understand how to process fights.

3. To educate readers on how not to make a regrettable incident become another regrettable incident.

Summary

This chapter discusses another mistake we make as a couple: stewing about the fight which means apologizing too fast before we understand what we're apologizing for or not processing the fight, the need for us to move in instead of trying to, the need to process fights, what happens when fights are not processed, and how to know that you need to address past events. It further discusses how we can process fights, the key to successful processing (reality and valid), how to move forward after conflict, steps to process a fight (feeling, realities, triggers, responsibility, and constructive planning), and some pitfalls to watch out for when you want to repair right.

Lessons

1. Our points of friction can become doorways to understanding each other better and becoming more connected, and more intimate.

2. A regrettable incident can become another regrettable incident.

3. Fights that go unprocessed force a wedge between the two of you either in the form of more conflict or in the form of less connection and avoidance.

4. When we don't repair after a bad fight, those wounds endure.

5. To understand what happened and to repair the hurt that was done, really have to understand what our partner saw, heard, and felt even if it's different from what we experienced during the incident.

6. Don't leap right into processing immediately after the fight.

7. A trigger is an event from the past, from your life before this relationship that generated a similar set of emotions.

8. Our conflicts are endless mirrors of our deeper humanity. They compel us to see and accept the full and complex humanity of our partner both the wonderful parts and the deeply human flaws.

Questions

1. How can the differences in the nature of a couple's job contribute to their conflict, using Molly and Selena as case study?

_____

_____

_____

_____

_____

_____

2. Why is it important to address and process conflicts instead of trying to "just move on"?

_____

_____

_____

_____

_____

_____

3. According to the chapter, how does the Zeigarnik effect relate to unresolved conflicts in relationships?

_____

_____

_____

_____

_____

_____

4. What are the steps to successfully processing a fight or conflict in a relationship, as described in the chapter?

_____

_____

_____

_____

_____

_____

5. Why is it significant for both partners to acknowledge that their perceptions and experiences of a conflict when processing a fight?

_____

_____

_____

_____

_____

_____

6. From your point of view, why is it important to validate each other's experiences in a relationship, even if you don't agree with them?

_____

_____

_____

_____

_____

_____

7. What are the consequences of apologizing immediately after a fight without understanding the full impact of your actions?

_____

_____

_____

_____

_____

_____

_____

8. How can we effectively move forward after a conflict in a relationship?

_____

_____

_____

_____

_____

_____

_____

9. How does triggers escalate conflicts in a relationship and how does understanding each other's triggers contribute to healing the conflict?

_____

_____

_____

_____

_____

_____

10. Considering the chapter, what are the potential pitfalls we need to watch out for when engaging in the repair process?

_____

_____

_____

_____

_____

_____

_____

Made in the USA
Coppell, TX
28 November 2024

41130635R00035